the spiritual and corporal
works of mercy

Coloring & Activity Book

Written by
Christina Wegendt

Illustrated by
Teresa Mossi

Pauline
BOOKS & MEDIA

Printed and published in the U.S.A. by Pauline Books & Media, 50 Saint Pauls Avenue, Boston, MA 02130-3491.

www. pauline.org

Pauline Books & Media is the publishing house of the Daughters of St. Paul,
an international congregation of women religious serving the Church with the communications media.
1 2 3 4 5 6   08 07 06 05 04 03

Sometimes we see people who need help. It's easy to just walk by and forget about them. But that's not what Jesus asks us to do. Jesus has told us, "Whatever you do to other people, you do to me."

Our Catholic Church gives a special name to good deeds done for others. That name is **works of mercy.** Works of mercy are actions done out of love and care for other people. The Church gives us a list of fourteen works of mercy. Seven of them have to do with what we all need for our *bodies.* We call these the **corporal works of mercy.** The other seven have to do with what we all need for our inner self or *spirit.* We call these the **spiritual works of mercy.**

This list of the works of mercy can remind us to love one another as Jesus wants us to:

Corporal Works of Mercy	**Spiritual Works of Mercy**
1. To feed the hungry	1. To admonish the sinner
2. To give drink to the thirsty	2. To instruct the ignorant
3. To shelter the homeless	3. To counsel the doubtful
4. To clothe the naked	4. To comfort the sorrowful
5. To visit the sick	5. To bear wrongs patiently
6. To visit those in prison	6. To forgive all injuries
7. To bury the dead	7. To pray for the living and the dead

Steve's friends love to play basketball at his house. To make sure that everyone has a good time, no one is allowed to use bad language or say unkind things about others.

To **admonish the sinner means** to warn someone not to do something that is a sin. It can also mean telling someone in a nice way that he or she has done something wrong, so that the person won't do it again.

admonish the sinner

4

admonish the sinner

Miguel and his friends really enjoy playing hockey. Help Miguel the goalie to unscramble this list of cool things to say when you're playing hard with your friends:

sweemoa _____

raf tuo _____

cine thos _____

olco _____

ywa ot og_____

sye! _____

rifciret _____

regat _____

lal hirtg _____

answers: awesome
far out
nice shot
cool
way to go
yes!
terrific
great
all right

5

Amanda has played piano *all* her life…well, for a few years, anyhow. Her younger brother Patrick really wants to learn, too. So after school, Amanda takes Patrick and helps him practice the exercises in the first book of piano lessons. They practice every day, and Amanda is patient when Patrick makes mistakes. After all, Amanda knows what it's like to be learning the piano herself!

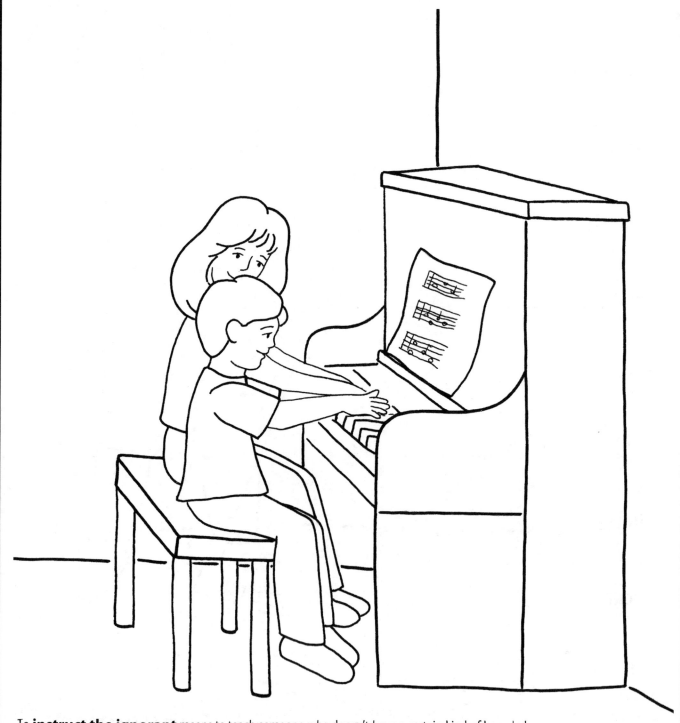

To **instruct the ignorant** means to teach someone who doesn't have a certain kind of knowledge.

instruct the ignorant

did you know

Here are some saintly fun-facts…for *your* instruction!

- Saint Isidore of Seville is the patron saint of cyberspace.

- Saint Genevieve was a vegetarian.

- There are at least 70 saints named John!

- Saint Veronica's real name was not Veronica! No one knows her real name, so we call her "Veronica," which means, "true image," since Jesus left his image on her veil when she dried his face on his way to Calvary.

- Saint Stanislaus walked 350 miles in order to enter a seminary in Rome!

- One of the first and greatest scientists was also a saint—Saint Albert the Great.

- Saint Fiacre is the patron saint of cab drivers.

- Saint John Gualbert almost murdered someone in revenge. He stopped just in time, forgave the person, and left to live in a monastery where he spent his life praying and working.

- Saint Joseph of Cupertino is the patron of astronauts.

Jamie tries to be a good listener when her friends or brother or sister have a problem. She knows she doesn't have all the answers, so she makes sure to say a quick prayer when someone needs her help or has to make a good decision.

To **counsel the doubtful** means to give good advice to a person who is not sure what to do or to believe.

counsel the doubtful

counsel the doubtful

Mark and Aaron have been assigned a huge book to read for English class. On top of that, they're practicing for a really big game. Their friend Neal has already read the book. "You don't have to read it," Neal says. "I can tell you all about it. That way you'll have more time for soccer practice."

Mark and Aaron aren't sure what to do. Write here what you would tell them:

When someone is sad or having a tough time, it's a really good idea to say a prayer with him or her and to share some time with the person.

To **comfort the sorrowful** means to try to cheer up and console someone who is sad or suffering in any way.

comfort the sorrowful

comfort the sorrowful

Ian's dog Rusty died a few days ago. His friend Nicole knows how much Ian misses Rusty, so she decides to give him a call to cheer him up. Which phone should Nicole use?

Chris and Anne were both asked by their teacher to help clean the chalk-boards after school. When school let out, Anne stood in the hall and talked to her friends about their plans for the evening, leaving Chris to clean the boards all by himself. Instead of losing his temper, Chris decided to act fairly and avoid an argument. He cleaned half of the boards. When he was finished, he said goodbye to his classmates in the hall and told Anne that she could do her share of the job when she was finished talking to her friends.

Homework:

Math p. 42

Spelling Unit 8

Science pp. 36-41

To **bear wrongs patiently** means to try not to get upset about the unjust things other people may do or say to us. (They might not even realize that they've done something wrong.) When someone does or says something against us, we can ask Jesus to help us to know how to act.

bear wrongs patiently

bear wrongs patiently

Have you ever been wronged? What exactly is a "wrong" anyway? A mistake on a math test? No. A "wrong" occurs when someone treats you unfairly. In the Old Testament story of Daniel in the lions' den, Daniel was wronged by being punished, even though he hadn't committed a crime. But Daniel didn't fight back, although he must have felt very upset.

WHAT DO YOU DO TO KEEP YOUR COOL?

Write here some things you can do to keep *your* cool when you feel upset or angry:

_____

_____

_____

_____

_____

_____

_____

_____

Forgiveness is tough. Sometimes people can make you really sad or even angry. They might not even realize how much they've hurt you. But holding grudges isn't the answer.

Take a look at Psalm 103 to see how God forgives us!

"For as high as the heavens are above the earth,

so wonderful is God's kindness toward those who love him.

As far as the east is from the west, so far has he placed our sins from us."

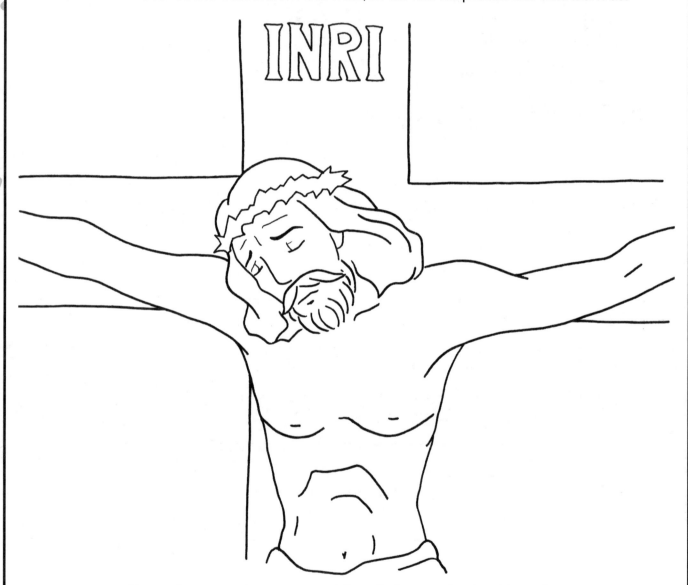

From the cross Jesus prayed for all those who had hurt him:

"Father, forgive them."

To **forgive all injuries** means to pardon those who have hurt us in any way.

forgive all injuries

Saint Peter once asked Jesus a very good question: How many times do we have to forgive people who hurt us? Once? Twice? Three times if they're *really* sorry?

Solve the puzzle below to find out what Jesus told Peter!

One Sorry Puzzle!

1/2 of **1000**   _____

minus **12**   _____

plus **6**   _____

minus **4** =   _____

answer:

490! Jesus meant that we should keep on forgiving no matter what!

On All Souls' Day, November 1ˢᵗ, Josh and Tamera go to Mass and pray for all people who have died. They also remember to pray for their families and their friends.

Join us for
a special
Mass on
All Souls' Day!

To **pray for the living and the dead** means to remember to pray for all people— those whom we know and love and those people who might have no one to pray for them.

pray for **living** and the **dead**

pray for the living and the dead

Everyone needs prayers! Mary, Jesus' mother, loves to listen to our prayers for others. She brings them all to Jesus.

GRANDPA

Holy Mary, Mother of God, pray for us sinners now and at the hour of our death. Amen.

Eric knows that there are many people in the world who don't have enough to eat. In fact, some people in his own city are hungry. When his parish holds its annual food drive to collect canned goods, Eric asks his mom if he can bring something to donate, too. Later, his parents take him to the soup kitchen where he helps out.

To **feed the hungry** means to help people who don't have enough to eat. We can give them food or money to buy food. We can also help serve food to homeless persons.

feed the hungry

feed the hungry

Eric has two nickels, a dime, three quarters, and four pennies. He wants to spend the money on an item to donate to the food drive at his parish. What is the most expensive item he can afford?

TODAY'S SPECIALS:

gallon of milk $1.99

mushroom soup $.99

bananas $.69 per pound

answer:
dnos

Tina's family has been working out in the yard all day long. She knows that everyone is hot and tired, so she decides to get them all a nice cold drink!

To **give drink to the thirsty** means helping those who don't have enough to drink. Besides being kind to the people around us, we can give money to help people in places where there isn't enough clean water to drink.

give drink to the thirsty

give drink to the thirsty

What do you suppose Tina will give her family?

Connect the dots below to discover the special drink she made.

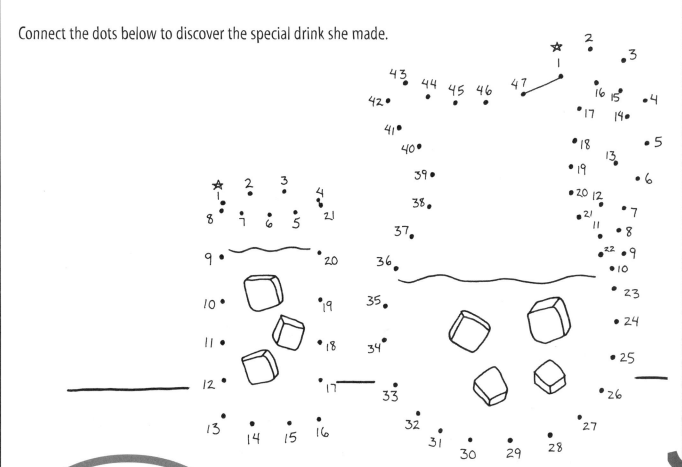

Whenever Stuart outgrows his clothes, he saves them. Then he and his parents take them to a thrift center run by the parishes in his town. That way other kids can enjoy all his favorite outfits!

Do you also have clothes that no longer fit you? Ask your mom and dad to give them to an organization that collects clothes for families in need.

To **clothe the naked** means to help provide clothes for the people who need them most.

clothe the naked

clothe the naked

Elizabeth of Hungary was a queen who lived long ago. She loved the poor. She often helped them by performing the works of mercy, including making sure that they had enough clothes to wear. Now Elizabeth is honored as a saint.

Color this picture of Saint Elizabeth giving a warm cloak to a young woman.

Noell's next-door-neighbor, Mrs. Dubbins, is a widow. Her son has to live out of town because of his job. Mrs. Dubbins usually stays at home because she doesn't drive and has difficulty walking very far. Noell often stops by to visit. Sometimes they work together in Mrs. Dubbins' garden. Sometimes they just sit and talk.

To **visit the imprisoned** means to take time to be with or to do something kind for someone who is no longer free to do certain things or go certain places. We say that a person who is in jail is imprisoned. But elderly or sick people who can't leave their homes are also imprisoned in a different way because they can no longer do all the things they used to do.

visit the imprisoned

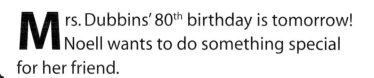

Mrs. Dubbins' 80th birthday is tomorrow! Noell wants to do something special for her friend.

In the space below, draw a picture of a gift that Noell could give to Mrs. Dubbins on this special day.

Hernando and Tyler are excited! They're going on the St. Francis Inn Walk-a-Thon. By taking part in the walk-a-thon they will help raise money to provide food and a place to sleep for people without a home.

To **shelter the homeless** means to try to do whatever we can to help people who have no house to live in.

shelter the homeles

shelter the homeless

Did you know that there's a saint who was homeless? His name is Saint Benedict Joseph Labre. He traveled all over Europe visiting many great shrines and churches. He often slept outdoors, and he rarely accepted money from the generous people who offered to help him. It just goes to show that to become a saint all we really need is love for God and one another!

Follow the maze below to take Saint Benedict Joseph on a pilgrimage through Europe! Make sure to visit each church along the way!

Start

Finish

Brittany's friend Kathy broke her leg this spring. Brittany knows that Kathy wishes she could be playing softball, so Brittany visits once in a while, and they play board games together outside.

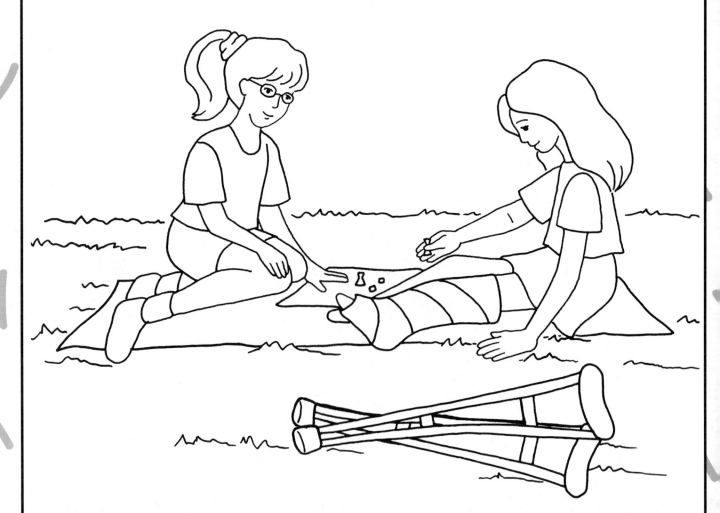

To **visit the sick** means to spend time with persons who are not feeling well. We can cheer them up by showing that we love and care for them.

visit the sick

visit the sick

Have you even been sick or hurt and had someone special to you come and visit? It can make you feel a lot better really quick!

Draw a picture below showing one of these special times.

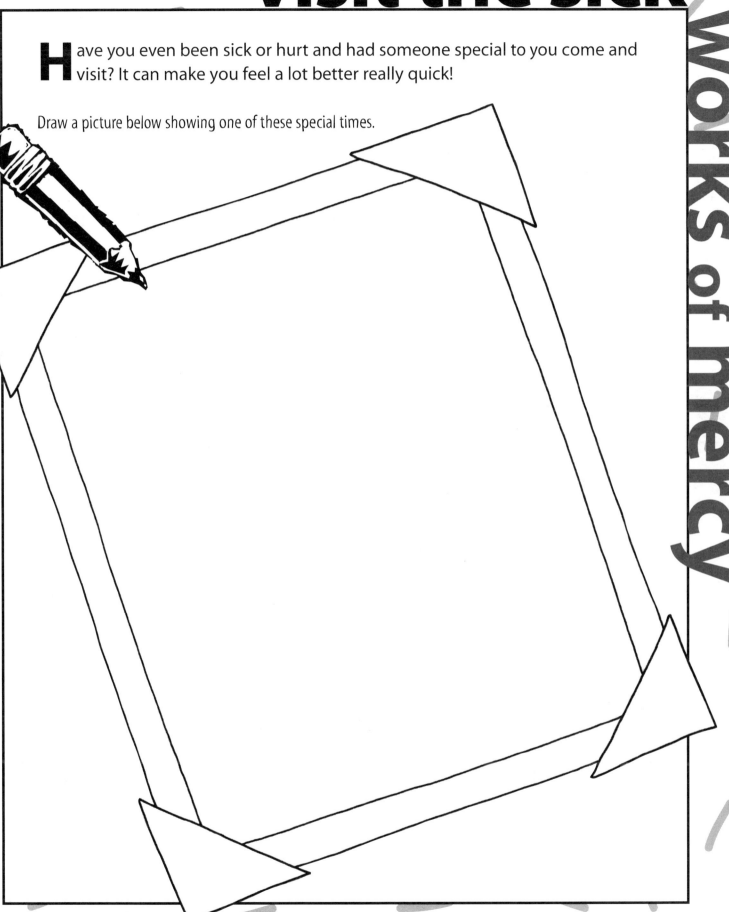

Connie's grandfather died last week, and Connie misses him very much. Many of her friends and classmates decided to attend the funeral. They want to pray for Connie's grandfather and for Connie and her family.

Connie's best friend, Robyn, tells her, "I know how much you must miss your grandfather. When I went to Mass on Sunday I prayed for him and for you."

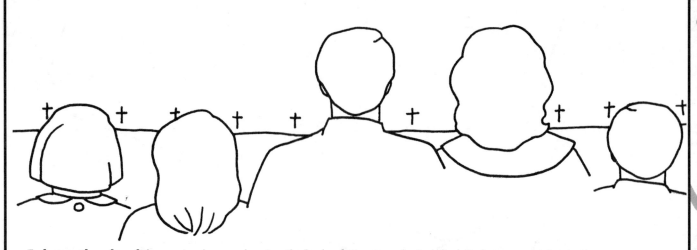

To **bury the dead** does not only mean burying the body of a person who has died. It also means going to the funeral Mass if we're able to. At that special Mass we pray together for the person and for his or her family.

bury the dead

There is a special prayer that we can say for people who have died. It's called *Eternal Rest.*

Color this picture of Jesus and try to learn the Eternal Rest prayer below it by heart. Hang the finished picture in your room. It will remind you to say the prayer often.

Eternal rest grant unto them, O Lord, and let perpetual light shine upon them. May they rest in peace. Amen

works of mercy

Pauline
BOOKS & MEDIA

The Daughters of St. Paul operate book and media centers at the following addresses.
Visit, call or write the one nearest you today, or find us on the World Wide Web, www.pauline.org

CALIFORNIA
3908 Sepulveda Blvd, Culver City, CA 90230   310-397-8676
5945 Balboa Avenue, San Diego, CA 92111   858-565-9181
46 Geary Street, San Francisco, CA 94108   415-781-5180
FLORIDA
145 S.W. 107th Avenue, Miami, FL 33174   305-559-6715
HAWAII
1143 Bishop Street, Honolulu, HI 96813   808-521-2731
Neighbor Islands call: 800-259-8463
ILLINOIS
172 North Michigan Avenue, Chicago, IL 60601   312-346-4228
LOUISIANA
4403 Veterans Memorial Blvd, Metairie, LA 70006   504-887-7631
MASSACHUSETTS
885 Providence Hwy, Dedham, MA 02026   781-326-5385
MISSOURI
9804 Watson Road, St. Louis, MO 63126   314-965-3512
NEW JERSEY
561 U.S. Route 1, Wick Plaza, Edison, NJ 08817   732-572-1200
NEW YORK
150 East 52nd Street, New York, NY 10022   212-754-1110
78 Fort Place, Staten Island, NY 10301   718-447-5071
PENNSYLVANIA
9171-A Roosevelt Blvd, Philadelphia, PA 19114   215-676-9494
SOUTH CAROLINA
243 King Street, Charleston, SC 29401   843-577-0175
TENNESSEE
4811 Poplar Avenue, Memphis, TN 38117   901-761-2987
TEXAS
114 Main Plaza, San Antonio, TX 78205   210-224-8101
VIRGINIA
1025 King Street, Alexandria, VA 22314   703-549-3806

CANADA
3022 Dufferin Street, Toronto, Ontario, Canada M6B 3T5   416-781-9131
1155 Yonge Street, Toronto, Ontario, Canada M4T 1W2   416-934-3440

¡También somos su fuente para libros, videos y música en español!